AnimalWays

Dolphins

Animalways

Dolphins

DAN GREENBERG

BENCHMARK BOOKS

MARSHALL CAVENDISH
NEW YORK

With special thanks to Paul Sieswerda of the New York Aquarium
for his expert reading of this manuscript.

Benchmark Books
Marshall Cavendish
99 White Plains Road
Tarrytown, NY 10591-9001
www.marshallcavendish.com

Text copyright © 2004 by Dan Greenberg
Illustrations copyright © 2004 by Ka Botzis
Diagrams by Daniel Roode
Diagrams copyright © 2004 by Marshall Cavendish Corporation

All Internet sites were available and accurate when sent to press.

Library of Congress Cataloging-in-Publication Data
Greenberg, Daniel A.
Dolphins / by Dan Greenberg.
p. cm. — (Animalways)
Includes bibliographical references and index (p.   ).
Contents: Mysterious travelers—What is a dolphin?—Dolphin habitats—Dolphins up
close—Dolphins in action—The life of a dolphin—Dolphins today and tomorrow.
ISBN 0-7614-1576-9
1. Dolphins—Juvenile literature. [1. Dolphins.] I. Title. II. Series.
QL737.C4G738 2003 599.53—dc21 2002155246

Photo Research by Candlepants Incorporated

Cover Photo: Corbis/Craig Tuttle

The photographs in this book are used by permission and through the courtesy of: *Corbis*:
Stuart Westmoreland, 9; The Purcell Team, 13, 74; Chris Abraham, 20; Stephen Frink, 23,
41; Gustavo Tomsich, 28; Lowell Georgia, 39; David A. Northcott, 53; Craig Tuttle, 63, 71;
Michele Westmoreland, 69; James L. Amos, 83; Amos Nachoum, 85; Richard A. Cooke,
90; Richard T. Nowitz, 102; *The Kobal Collection/MGM*: 10–11; *Animals/Animals*: James
Watt, 15, 34–35, 61, 86; John Chellman, 35 (center); Zig Leszczynski, 50, 67; Bob Cranston,
75; Gerard Lacz, 87; *Space and Naval Warfare Systems Center San Diego*, 17; *American
Museum of Natural History Library/Photo #325244 by Rota*: 25; *Illustration by Carl Buell,
from www.neoucom.edu/Depts/Anat/Pakicetid.html*, 27; *Photo Researchers Inc.*, Richard
Ellis, 30; Francois Gohier, 34 (top), (left), (right), 44, 54, 60, 66, 79, back cover; Gregory
Ochocki, 35 (lower right), 48; Lawrence Naylor, 57; Jacana/Gerard Soury, 58; Art Wolfe,
64; Tom Mc Hugh, 73; Dolphin Institute, 77; Jeff Rotman, 81; Herve Donnezan, 95; Simon
Fraser, 97, 99; *Brandon D. Cole*, 35 (top); *Getty Images*: National Geographic Collection/
Joel Sartore, 45; The Image Bank/Stuart Westmoreland, 47; *Robert L. Pitman/Seapics.com*, 93.

Printed in China

1 3 5 6 4 2

Contents

Animal Kingdom

CNIDARIANS

coral

ARTHROPODS
(animals with jointed limbs and external skeleton)

MOLLUSKS

squid

CRUSTACEANS

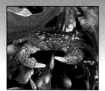

crab

ARACHNIDS

spider

INSECTS

grasshopper

MYRIAPODS

centipede

CARNIVORES

lion

SEA MAMMALS

DOLPHINS

PRIMATES

orangutan

HERBIVORES
(5 orders)

elephant

PHYLA

ANNELIDS

earthworm

CHORDATES
(animals with
a dorsal
nerve chord)

ECHINODERMS

starfish

SUB PHYLA

VERTEBRATES
(animals with a
backbone)

CLASSES

FISH

fish

BIRDS

gull

MAMMALS

AMPHIBIANS

frog

REPTILES

snake

ORDERS

RODENTS

squirrel

INSECTIVORES

mole

MARSUPIALS

koala

SMALL MAMMALS
(several orders)

bat

1 Mysterious Travelers

> CHEERFUL AND CHARMING
> WONDERFUL AND WISE
> THE DOLPHIN IS INTELLIGENT
> YOU CAN SEE IT IN ITS EYES
>
> YOU CAN HEAR IT IN ITS VOICE
> IN THE SMOOTHNESS OF ITS SKIN
> BUT CAN WE KNOW FOR SURE WHAT LURKS
> BENEATH THE DOLPHIN'S GRIN?
>
> WHEN YOU OBSERVE A DOLPHIN
> NO MATTER WHAT YOU DO
> KEEP IN MIND THAT AS YOU WATCH
> THE DOLPHIN WATCHES YOU!

What is it about dolphins? Are they really as cheerful, charming, wonderful, and downright amazing as they appear to be? In fact, dolphins are very special creatures. They're friendly, curious, highly intelligent, and possess a dazzling array of talents and abilities. The ancient Greeks thought so highly of these "smooth and gentle creatures" that they made it

DOLPHINS SEEM TO HAVE A NATURAL SMILE, BUT THIS EXPRESSION HAS LITTLE TO SAY ABOUT THEIR INNER FEELINGS.

a crime to harm one. If a Greek killed a dolphin, he or she was put on trial for murder! Today, dolphins are loved around the world. There are Web sites, television shows, research centers, and spiritual healing programs devoted to dolphins.

Each year, thousands of visitors travel to places like the Dolphin Research Center in Grassy Key, Florida, to participate in swim-with-a-dolphin programs. In ocean theme parks like SeaWorld, which has locations in Florida, California, and Texas, dolphins are the headliners of the shows, thrilling audiences with their athletic leaps, spins, and twirls. On television and in movies, dolphins have also been stars. The most famous dolphin character was probably Flipper, who appeared in a weekly television series in the 1960s and in films in the 1990s. The dolphins used in the first television series were trained by Ric O'Barry.

Remarkable as they were, even Flipper's exploits, such as catching "bad guys" and rescuing victims, take a backseat to the real-life feats of dolphins such as Pelorus Jack, a Risso's dolphin from New Zealand, and Fungie the Dingle Dolphin, a bottlenose from Ireland. Both creatures were completely wild, never having been trained by a human being. Yet, they were curious about people and drawn to make contact with them. From 1888 to 1912 Pelorus Jack became known throughout the South Seas for his bow-riding,

PERPHAPS THE MOST FAMOUS DOLPHIN OF THEM ALL, FLIPPER WAS A "FAMOUS" TELEVISION AND MOVIE STAR IN THE LATE TWENTIETH CENTURY.

boat-chasing, crowd-pleasing antics. Fungie is a more recent dolphin star. There is even a Web site that contains information on him. Since the 1990s, thousands of visitors have taken tour boat rides to see Fungie near his home in a harbor on the coast of Ireland. Fungie plays with swimmers, splashes boats, and performs leaps. Some say he prefers people and boats to other dolphins.

Why do people like dolphins so much? Being genial, charming, and entertaining like Fungie certainly is appealing. The dolphin's habit of interacting with the human species is well

known in seafaring communities. Stories of sailors, travelers, and fishers being helped by dolphins are numerous. Dolphins have rescued people from shark attacks, shipwrecks, accidents, and many other dire situations on the high seas.

Dolphins seem to have a knack for sensing and helping people in trouble. Their intuition raises an important question: just how smart are dolphins? Very smart. Though some people—especially pet owners—insist that dolphins are no brighter than cocker spaniels, scientists and field-workers who have spent time with dolphins are deeply impressed with their wide-ranging mental abilities.

Dolphin Intelligence

Dolphins and other cetaceans (whales and porpoises) do have large brains—larger in proportion to body size than any other animal except humans and apes. Though a large brain does not guarantee mental ability, dolphins seem to display a keen intelligence in many aspects of their lives. In captivity, dolphins learn quickly and have an excellent memory for skills learned long ago. They also seem to have an extraordinary ability to interpret body language and emotions, moods and feelings—whether the individual is happy, impatient, uncomfortable, or upset. It is not surprising that dolphins in the wild are so socially perceptive given their complex social lives. The typical dolphin must keep track of dozens, perhaps even hundreds, of different relationships with its pod-mates.

Just about all of the traits described above suggest that dolphins are smart, but do they rival human beings in intelligence? Probably not, according to most researchers. But there are still many things about dolphins that people do not understand—sophisticated communication being one of them. Dolphins are

An up-close experience with a dolphin is something that most people never forget.

among the few organisms that may possess true language. They produce a rich variety of vocalizations that certainly *sound* like language. But are these whistles, yips, and pops truly a systematic form of communication, or are they just a complex variety of noises?

Researchers who have spent years trying to decipher dolphin "speech" have come to doubt that the sounds add up to a language.

Over the past thirty-five years researchers have investigated what is known as a dolphin's signature whistle—a unique pattern of sounds made by an individual dolphin. It is thought that dolphins use their signature whistle to identify themselves. Are signature whistles names? Recent research has cast some doubt on whether signature whistles represent names or simply the voice pattern of an individual dolphin. In any event, this research is a step toward uncovering just how sophisticated dolphin communication is.

Some people claim that dolphin intelligence goes beyond that of human beings and that dolphins are highly advanced organisms possessing knowledge and spiritual wisdom of benefit to the human race. Dolphins are said to possess powerful mental abilities, including telepathy (mental communication) extrasensory perception (ESP), X-ray vision, sonar (the use of sound waves to detect objects), and the power to heal people with serious physical and psychological disorders.

Most of these claims are, at best, unproven. However, dolphins do possess a type of inner sonar, called echolocation, which they use to navigate the ocean depths. A dolphin uses echolocation to send out sound waves to bounce off distant objects and then judge the shape and distance of the objects by the speed and quality of the echoes. The sounds the dolphin sends out are clicks. Since the clicks can penetrate objects, a

Atlantic spotted dolphins travel in a variety of group sizes—from just a couple to hundreds of individuals.

dolphin can sense whether an object is solid or hollow—which, when you think about it, is a form of "X-ray vision."

The claim that dolphins have telepathy stems in part from observations of large groups of oceanic dolphins swimming in formation. The dolphins maneuver in perfect unison without any outward hint of communication among the pod members. Even in small performing groups, the dolphins do the same thing, instantly and effortlessly, without any visible or vocal signal. How do they do it?

The mechanism behind dolphin "instant communication" is one of the things about dolphins that puzzles scientists. Less puzzling are the claims that dolphins possess such talents as healing powers, spiritual wisdom, and ESP. Most scientists doubt that dolphins possess any of these. Though dolphins react to gestures, body posture, muscle tension, and other nonverbal cues, their responsiveness does not suggest that they can cure an illness, read a person's mind, or locate wounds, broken bones, and other disturbances in a person's body. Still, many people believe that dolphins can work miracles. One story tells of a dolphin who detected something unusual in a woman's abdomen. Had she undergone surgery recently? the trainer asked. The woman insisted that she was perfectly all right, but two weeks later she wrote back to say she had found out that she was pregnant. The dolphin had apparently detected her condition before she knew about it herself!

Dolphin enthusiasts like Horace Dobbs believe that dolphins have special healing powers for mental disorders. Dobbs tells of a man who had been depressed for years, only to meet up with a dolphin named Simo. He instantly began speaking to the dolphin and playing with it. Dobbs attributes the man's recovery to Simo.

With their high intelligence, sophisticated sonar, swimming

UNDERWATER, DOLPHINS CAN DO THINGS THAT PEOPLE CANNOT. THIS DOLPHIN IS DETECTING AND MARKING EXPLOSIVE UNDERSEA MINES. THE U.S. NAVY'S DOLPHIN PROJECT HAS LASTED FOR MORE THAN FORTY YEARS.

and diving abilities, and intuition, dolphins are well suited to carry out military missions too dangerous for human beings. Accordingly, in the 1960s the U.S. Navy began training dolphins for military missions. For more than forty years, U.S. Navy trainers have taught dolphins to do such things as find and mark underwater mines and detect enemy divers. Though the program was successful, federal funding was cut in the late 1980s and the number of dolphins used was reduced for a number of years. Now, the U.S. Navy dolphin program is back in full swing. Dolphins are considered the best way to locate underwater mines—the primary danger to U.S. ships.

Many people believe that dolphins should not be used to

aid the military, or to do tricks. Dolphin rights advocates believe that dolphins are more than just animals. They feel that dolphins, like people, are self-aware beings that deserve better than to live in a caged space and perform tricks for a living. Awareness of dolphin rights has forced aquariums, dolphin shows, and dolphin research programs to rethink their priorities and set some captive dolphins free. Ric O'Barry, the trainer of television's Flipper dolphins, is one of the converts. Even after spending years training dolphins, O'Barry became convinced that it was wrong to force animals of such subtle intelligence and grace to perform tricks. O'Barry is now against any kind of treatment that is demeaning to dolphins.

How self-aware are dolphins? Recent experiments at the New York Aquarium have demonstrated that two bottlenose dolphins named Presley and Tab were able to accomplish something that only human beings and some great apes had ever accomplished: they recognized themselves in a mirror. Each dolphin was marked with an ink spot on different parts of its body. After an ink spot was applied the dolphins spent considerable time in front of the mirror examining the location where the spot was painted. When a spot was erased and a new spot painted in a different location, the dolphins spent more time observing that new location. These experiments showed that dolphins, like human beings, are aware of themselves.

In the Company of Dolphins: Up Close and Personal

The first thing you notice about dolphins in the wild is how confident they are. The water is the dolphin's home, its element. Dolphins glide through the water easily.

Not being afraid or on edge does not mean the dolphin is not curious or excited about a visitor. Curiosity may be one of the most distinctive of all dolphin traits. Many (but not all) dolphin species are interested in people. There are probably as many as ten dolphin species that are especially curious about people—the most well known being the bottlenose dolphin. Some bottlenoses, like Fungie the Dingle Dolphin of Ireland, never seem to tire of approaching boats and encountering people. It should be said, however, that many boat-loving dolphins may be more interested in the watercrafts than the people inside of them. This is because dolphins like to bow ride and wake ride. They hitchhike on the waves that spill from the bow and track of a boat and with little effort speed alongside it.

In the Company of Dolphins: Sounds, Touch, and Movement

One of the first things people notice in the company of dolphins is the sounds that they make. Below the first 65 feet (20 m) or so, oceans are largely without light. Because they spend a great deal of time in the dark, the dolphins' world is largely organized around sound. Indeed, a visitor to a dolphin's habitat is greeted by a great deal of noisy chatter: clicks, whistles, pops, yelps, pips, and squeals. Talk to dolphins and they talk back. Laugh and they laugh back— the ability of dolphins to mimic is well known. People who spend time with dolphins are struck by their playfulness and mischievous sense of humor. Dolphin trainers marvel over their different personalities and how much a dolphin seems to "train" the human, rather than the other way around. Much of the chatter and clicks that dolphins emit is produced for echolocation. Other sounds—whistles, squeals, pops—are used for other reasons.

Though the dolphin's world may be dominated by sound, its ability to express itself may be more dependent on touch than any other sense. In the wild, a pod of dolphins frequently nuzzles, nips, and makes body contact with one another. When people get close to dolphins they quickly come to appreciate how much dolphins communicate using body language, gestures, jumps, spins, postures, and writhing rhythms.

OTHER THAN SOUND, TOUCH IS PROBABLY THE MOST IMPORTANT OF THE DOLPHIN'S SENSES.

What do these movements signify? Researchers are just beginning to understand the importance of physical contact and gestures to dolphins. But if you doubt that physical gestures have any meaning, observe a few human conversations and note how much is communicated without words but by the tone of voice, hand motions, body posture, facial expressions, and eye contact.

Dolphin-to-dolphin communication probably depends more on nonverbal action than human communication does. Some scientists feel that gestures and movements are the keys to dolphin communication and that sounds are secondary. They theorize that dolphin communication is more like music than speech. It expresses mood, feelings, and other emotional states in a rhythmic, ever-shifting pattern rather than spelling out facts and ideas.

2 What Is a Dolphin?

People who think of dolphins as cute and cuddly are often surprised to learn that the creature that resembles them the most in behavior is the shark. Sharks and dolphins are both efficient, swift, and aggressive predators. Both often swim in the same waters and hunt for the same prey. There are times when dolphins and sharks "hang out" together. Are dolphins a kind of "friendly" shark?

When you look closely at the two animals, you see that they are decidedly different. Sharks, after all, are fish; dolphins are mammals. As fish, sharks breathe through gills and swim using a side-to-side motion. Dolphins breathe air through lungs and swim with an up-and-down motion.

Though dolphins and other cetaceans are frequently mislabeled as "fish," observers have known for thousands of years that they were actually mammals. The Greek philosopher Aristotle, for one, was well aware that a dolphin could not be a

THE DOLPHIN BODY IS PERFECTLY DESIGNED FOR FAST AND EFFICIENT UNDERWATER TRAVEL. ESTIMATES SHOW THAT DOLPHINS USE ONLY ONE-EIGHTH THE ENERGY TO SWIM THAT A HUMAN OLYMPIC SWIMMER USES. DOLPHINS CAN GO ABOUT AS FAST AS 34 MILES PER HOUR (55 KMH).

fish. He based his conclusion on the observation that dolphins, like other cetaceans, had to come up to the surface of the water every few minutes to breathe. But this raised other questions: If dolphins were fish, then what were they doing gulping air? And if dolphins were mammals, what were they doing in the water?

Traits of Mammals

They:

✔ Are warm-blooded (endothermic)
✔ Possess body hair
✔ Give birth to live young
✔ Feed on mother's milk when young

Dolphins have all of these traits except for body hair, which has been largely eliminated over time.

Evolution of Dolphins

How dolphins ended up in the water is the story of cetacean evolution. Fish live in the water because, evolutionarily speaking, they never left the water. Dolphins, on the other hand, are part of a group that left the water, colonized the land, and then returned to the water.

The first animals began to colonize the land some 400 million years ago. Arthropods and other invertebrates came first, followed by fishlike amphibians, reptiles, and other animals with backbones.

The first mammals appeared on land about 210 million years ago. At the dawn of the age of dinosaurs, these early mammals were pint-sized creatures no bigger than a modern-day hamster. Over the next 145 million years, as dinosaurs multiplied, grew to massive sizes, and became the dominant life-form on Earth, mammals largely stayed the same. Things did not change until the great extinction, about 65 million years ago. During this period thousands of animal species, including every dinosaur species, became extinct. Scientists believe that the extinctions were the result of a comet colliding with Earth.

With dinosaurs gone, the remaining mammals began to change rapidly, increasing in size in only a few million years and moving into habitats from which they had previously been excluded. As their numbers increased on land, mammals began to colonize niches in shallow water areas as well. This return to the water probably occurred in stages. The first mammals most likely entered the water for one of two reasons: either they were trying to chase down prey or they were trying to escape from predators. In any event, this new habitat proved to be rich in opportunity for mammals. There was an abundant source of food in the waters, and it was a good place to escape from enemies.

As time passed, mammal species evolved that could swim and maneuver efficiently in shallow water. Among these were the wolflike mesonychid condylarths, the possibly hoofed ancestors of modern cetaceans who lived about 53 million years

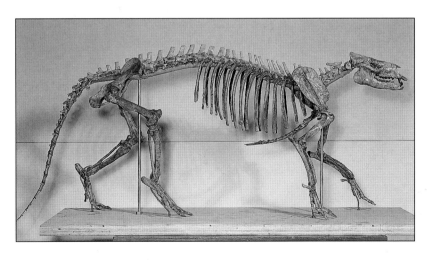

THE MESONYCHID CONDYLARTH WAS ABOUT 4.5 FEET (1.3 M) IN LENGTH. IT USED ITS LONG TAIL TO PADDLE THROUGH THE WATER, MUCH LIKE A MODERN-DAY OTTER.

TIMELINE

Million Years Ago	
210	Mammals and dinosaurs appear
70	Hoofed mammals begin to appear
66	End of dinosaurs
53	Mesonychid condylarths appear
47	The time of the *Hapalodectes*
46	*Pakicetus* appears
30	Toothed whales and baleen whales become separate species
24	Kentriodontidae appear
10	Delphinidae (modern dolphins) emerge

ago. *Mesonychids* were adept at pursuing fish and other aquatic prey in lagoons and other shallow coastal areas.

About 50 million years ago, the *mesonychids* gave rise to other hoofed cetacean ancestors, including the large, otterlike *Hapalodectes*, which sped through the water by tucking its legs under its body and beating its tail up and down. The trend, as the ancestors of cetaceans became more adapted to a life in water, was to become more streamlined, have less fur, and take on a thicker, more powerful tail and reduced, flipperlike limbs. By 46 million years ago, the 6.6–foot (2–m) long *Pakicetus* was probably the first true cetacean, an otterlike creature that seems to have lived exclusively in the water.

Over the 30 million years that followed *Pakicetus*, adaptations for efficiency in the water continued in a variety of cetacean ancestors. Front legs turned into flippers. Rear legs and body hair disappeared. Tails broadened and became attached to powerful swimming muscles. The nostrils for breathing migrated to the top of the head and became blowholes. Around 30 million

WAS *PAKICETUS* THE ORIGINAL CETACEAN ANCESTOR? DNA EVIDENCE SUGGESTS THAT IT WAS.

years ago, cetaceans split into two groups—the Mysticeti (baleen whales) and the Ondotoceti (toothed whales).

As time passed, baleen whales grew larger, while toothed whales stayed moderate in size. The reason for the size increase in one cetacean group and not in the other is largely a matter of feeding styles. Baleen whales, as bulk filter feeders, could afford to become as big as possible because they did not need to hunt down prey one by one. Toothed whales, on the other hand, needed speed and agility to catch up with fast, individual prey, and so they

DOLPHINS WERE WELL KNOWN TO THE ANCIENT GREEKS AND ROMANS. THE ROMANS REGARDED DOLPHINS AS MUSICAL CREATURES—PROBABLY BECAUSE OF THE SOUNDS THEY MADE.

tended to stay a moderate size. As toothed whales and hunters of individual prey, dolphins stayed small and nimble. Though dolphins grew to be larger than many mammal predators on land, they are still much smaller than their baleen cousins.

By 24 million years ago the Kentriodontidae became the forerunners of modern dolphins. These creatures seemed to have all the basic dolphin body structures and features. They were shaped much like modern dolphins and possessed echolocation systems. The family that includes modern oceanic dolphins, the Delphinidae, arose from the kentriodonts about 10 million years ago. Since then, changes in the dolphin body form and basic physiology have been minor.

Dolphin or Whale?

One might ask what seems like an overly simple question: is a dolphin a whale? Technically speaking, since all toothed cetaceans are whales, dolphins are whales, too. In general, size is the determining factor for whether a cetacean is called a whale. Cetaceans greater than 33 feet (10 m) are generally called whales. Cetaceans that measure between 8 to 26 feet (2.5 to 8 m) are called dolphins, or blackfish. Porpoises are the smallest cetaceans, generally less than 8 feet (2.5 m).

Dolphins themselves can be divided into three groups. The main group of oceanic dolphins are the Delphinidae. Of the thirty-three Delphinidae species, twenty-seven species are commonly referred to as dolphins. The other six Delphinidae are the blackfish—killer whales and pilot whales. Blackfish are nothing more than large, dark-colored dolphins. But their appearance and behavior are so distinct that they are often considered to be separate from the dolphin group.

In addition to the Delphinidae, there are also five species of

THIS CHINESE RIVER DOLPHIN IS ONE OF THE FIVE RIVER DOLPHIN SPECIES.

river dolphins and five porpoise species. The chart on page 31 shows how dolphins fit into the order of cetaceans. Dolphins are classified as toothed nonwhales to set them apart from the toothed cetaceans commonly referred to as whales.

Dolphin Groups

Dolphins are classified in a number of ways. It is generally agreed that the four nonwhale cetacean groups in the chart on page 31 are separate and distinct: oceanic dolphins, blackfish, river dolphins, and porpoises.

Delphinidae are referred to as the oceanic dolphins. All twenty-seven species of oceanic dolphins live in ocean habitats. However, within the oceans these dolphin species occupy different habitats, so they are further divided into two subgroups: open-ocean dolphins and coastal dolphins. Open-ocean dolphins

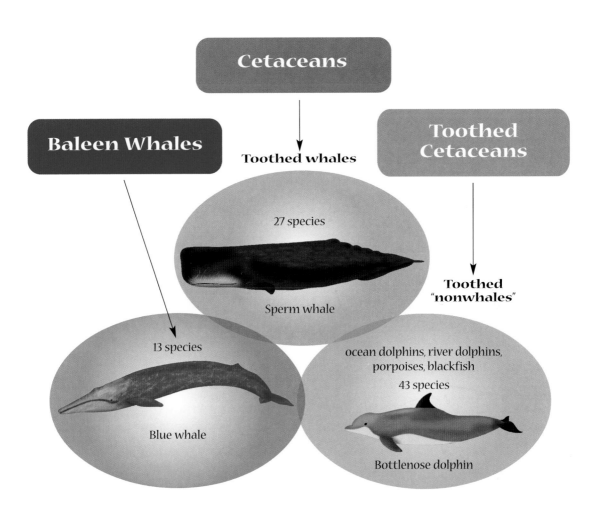

Cetaceans

Baleen Whales

Toothed whales

Toothed Cetaceans

27 species

Sperm whale

Toothed "nonwhales"

13 species

Blue whale

ocean dolphins, river dolphins, porpoises, blackfish

43 species

Bottlenose dolphin

Whales
Baleen whales	13 species, Example: Blue whale
Toothed whales	27 species, Example: Sperm whale
Total:	39 species

"Nonwhale" Toothed Cetaceans
Oceanic dolphins	27 species, Example: Bottlenose dolphin
Blackfish	6 species, Example: Pilot whale
River dolphins	5 species, Example: Boto
Porpoises	5 species, Example: Harbor porpoise
Total:	43 species

Dolphins

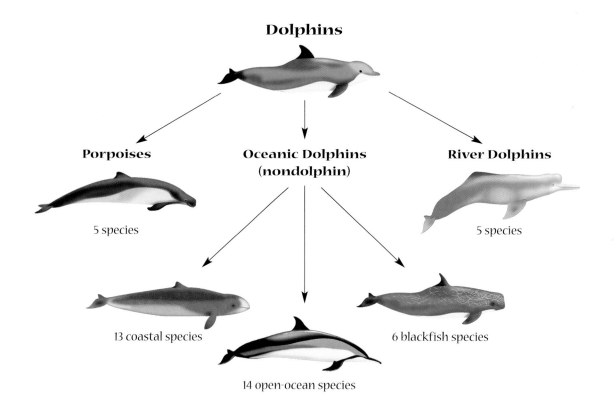

Porpoises
5 species

**Oceanic Dolphins
(nondolphin)**

River Dolphins
5 species

13 coastal species

6 blackfish species

14 open-ocean species

include such species as the spinner dolphin, Atlantic spotted dolphin, pantropical spotted dolphin, common dolphin, bottlenose dolphin, Pacific white-sided dolphin, and Risso's dolphin.

Coastal dolphins include the white-beaked dolphin, Atlantic white-sided dolphin, dusky dolphin, hump-backed dolphin, and Irrawaddy. There are fourteen open-ocean dolphins and thirteen coastal dolphins. Several species, such as the bottlenose and Atlantic spotted dolphin, inhabit both open ocean and coastal areas.

The river dolphins include boto from the Amazon, baiji from China's Yangtze River, susu from India, bhulan from Pakistan, and the franciscana, which inhabits river and coastal habitats.

Porpoises are generally smaller and less social than dolphins. Common porpoises include Dall's porpoise, the harbor

Dolphin Species

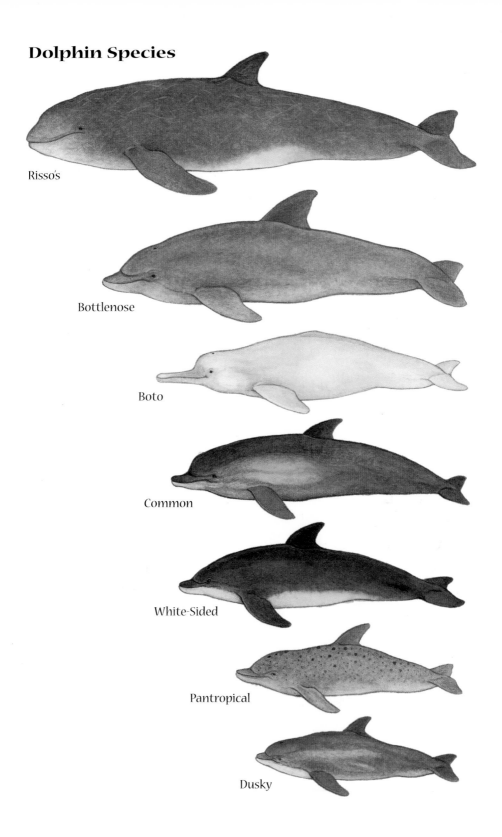

Risso's

Bottlenose

Boto

Common

White-Sided

Pantropical

Dusky

THE "SPOTTER" IS AN OPEN-OCEAN SPECIES, DISTINGUISHED BY ITS BRIGHT SPOTS.

THE COMMON DOLPHIN IS ANOTHER OPEN-OCEAN SPECIES, DISTINGUISHED BY ITS BRIGHT SIDE PATCH.

THE OPEN-OCEAN SPINNER DOLPHIN PUTS ON QUITE A SHOW. THESE DOLPHINS ARE EASILY RECOGNIZED BY THEIR LONG SNOUTS.

THE PACIFIC WHITE-SIDED DOLPHIN LIVES IN COASTAL REGIONS AND IS KNOWN AS AN EXTREMELY PLAYFUL AND FRIENDLY SPECIES.

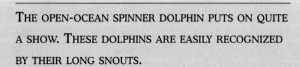

THE DUSKY DOLPHIN, A COASTAL COUSIN OF THE PACIFIC WHITE-SIDED DOLPHIN, SWIMS WITH ANOTHER COASTAL SPECIES, HECTOR'S DOLPHIN. MANY OTHER DOLPHINS SWIM TOGETHER AS WELL.

THE BOTTLENOSE DOLPHIN IS THE WORLD'S MOST WIDELY RECOGNIZED SPECIES.

THE AMAZON BOTO (SOMETIMES CALLED THE "PINK PORPOISE") IS PERHAPS THE STRANGEST-LOOKING DOLPHIN OF ALL.

porpoise, the finless porpoise, and the vaquita. Many people confuse the terms "dolphin" and "porpoise." In most cases, porpoises are mistakenly labeled as dolphins simply because dolphins, as the more social and outgoing of the two, are likely to be seen more often than the more secretive porpoises.

The Dolphin Adaptation

A look at the dolphin's anatomy highlights the changes that have taken place in the millions of years since their hoofed ancestors turned into animals that spent their entire lives in the water. Returning to the water presented cetaceans with five basic problems: staying warm, moving efficiently, maintaining inner salt balance, withstanding underwater pressure, and breathing.

The dolphin solved the problem of staying warm in a way that might at first seem unexpected. Living in a cold environment, you might think that dolphins would have increased the amount of fur on their bodies. Instead, cetaceans did the opposite. The outside of the dolphin's body is bare and smooth. Unlike seals, otters, and some other marine mammals, dolphins have lost all traces of their fur. How do dolphins stay warm? Like other cetaceans, dolphins have developed a thick layer of body fat, or blubber, that insulates them against the cold and gives them an energy source when food is scarce.

The second problem that cetaceans faced living in an underwater environment was movement—how to get around in a medium that is so much more dense than air. To solve this problem, dolphins took on a streamlined shape. Dolphin skin is smooth, and a dolphin's body is rounded and contoured to slip easily through the water. Front legs turned into flippers. The neck is short and the head seems to flow into the shoulders. The rear legs disappeared. A new structure, the tail fluke, appeared and

Dolphin Skeleton

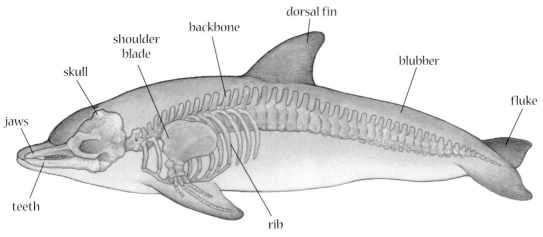

became the dolphin's primary means of locomotion.

Because they are mammals dolphins have a swimming style different from that of fish and most other underwater creatures. Fish undulate side-to-side, wriggling their tails and bodies horizontally. Their fins serve as paddles. Their vertical tails serve as propellers and steering rudders.

Dolphins are up-and-down swimmers. Propulsion is provided by the dolphin's powerful tail fluke while they use their fins for steering. The fluke itself is oriented on a horizontal plane. Slow-motion films show that a dolphin's up-and-down swimming motion more closely resembles the running style of a speeding land mammal—such as a dog or a cheetah—than it does of a fast-swimming fish such as a tuna. The animal's flexible spine pumps up and down, transferring its power to the broad tail.

The third challenge to the dolphin is to maintain salt balance in a marine environment. Land and freshwater animals can take in drinking water whenever they need to. Living in the salty ocean, dolphins and other cetaceans do not have this luxury. Scientists do not completely understand how cetaceans

Dolphin Organs

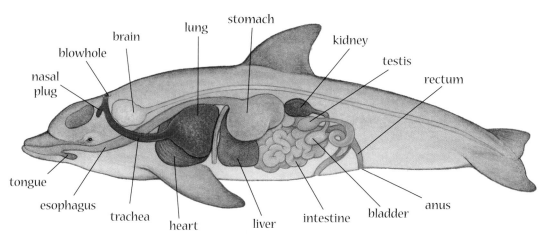

maintain the proper balance of salt in the body, but somehow they manage this from the food they take in and the action of their kidneys' filtration system.

Pressure is the fourth problem that dolphins face in the undersea environment. On land, mammals do not need to worry about pressure from air. Water is extremely heavy, and its weight takes its toll on underwater creatures. Every 32.8 feet (10 m) in depth that an animal goes down increases the amount of pressure on the body by 1 atmosphere, the standard amount of pressure that is felt at sea level. (One atmosphere means that at a depth of 10 meters, the pressure is 2 atmospheres, at a 20–meter depth is 3 atmospheres, and so on.) Solid body structures, such as flippers, are not much affected by pressure because there is no empty space to squeeze. Hollow structures, however, such as lungs, get squeezed as a dolphin dives. To minimize pressure effects, the dolphin's skeletal ribs "float" in its body cavity—instead of being rigidly attached to a sternum bone like the ribs of land mammals. These floating ribs allow the dolphin to collapse its

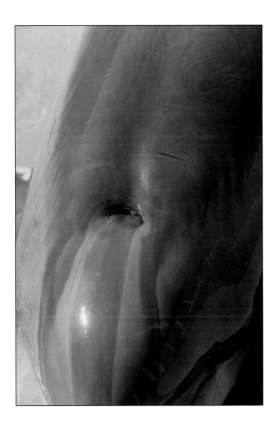

lungs during dives and not suffer ill effects from underwater pressure. Dolphins have also reduced hollow spaces in their bones so they can dive freely without suffering the effects of the increased pressure.

The final problem that dolphins needed to solve to live underwater was breathing. Fish and other aquatic creatures take in oxygen out of the water through gills. Without gills, dolphins must come to the surface and breathe air every few minutes. Gas exchange in the dolphin's lungs is much more efficient than it is for humans. Humans replenish only about 10 percent of lung volume during each breath. Dolphins, on the other hand, replenish about 80 percent of their lung volume, meaning that after a few short breaths their lungs are full of fresh air and they are ready to submerge again.

3 Dolphin Habitats

Dolphins live in three habitats: the open ocean, coastal regions, and river systems. The dolphin's body shape, feeding behavior, and way of life differ depending on where it lives. Open-ocean dolphins are generally fast and sleek. Dolphins that live in shallow water tend to be stouter, less streamlined, and not as fast. River dolphins are the slowest swimmers.

Ocean Habitats

As with land, beneath the surface oceans are home to a variety of environments and local "neighborhoods." Ocean habitats are organized horizontally by their nearness to land and vertically by depth.

Horizontally, the ocean is divided into four zones. The intertidal zone is the closest to land. It consists of beaches, marshes, and river mouths touched by the rise and fall of the tides. During low tides, large parts of the intertidal zone may be exposed to the air. During high tides, most or all of the intertidal zone is under water.

AS AIR-BREATHERS, DOLPHINS ARE NEVER FAR FROM THE SURFACE. LIGHT IS ONLY AVAILABLE IN THE UPPERMOST REGIONS OF THE OCEAN.

The continental shelf is the region that extends from the coastline out to about 45 miles (72 km). The continental shelf gently slopes to a depth of about 660 feet (200 m) and is rich with plant and animal life. As the shelf extends farther out, it ends in a steep drop-off. This continental edge, or third zone, flattens out as it reaches the fourth ocean zone, the abyssal plain, or ocean bottom. The ocean bottom has an average depth of 13,000 feet (4 km) and in its troughs reaches depths of 35,630 feet (10,860 m).

The properties of each ocean habitat largely depend on two things, sunlight and temperature. With respect to sunlight, keep in mind that water is not a completely transparent medium. At a depth of 1,312 feet (400 m), seawater blocks out sunlight completely. Below this depth the ocean is cast in darkness. Water temperature does not vary as much as light. The ocean settles in layers with the warm water on the topmost level. Warm water occupies the uppermost layer for two reasons—first, the upper layers are closest to the sun's energy, and second, warm water rises because it is less dense than cold water. Cold water, being denser, sinks. Generally, the lower you go in depth, the colder the water.

The Open Ocean

The largest ocean habitat is probably the one most unfamiliar to people who have not spent time on the high seas. The open ocean is a vast, watery place where everything is exposed. All predators in this place are also potential prey. Dolphins hunt in the open ocean, but they are also hunted there by sharks and killer whales. Even the sharks must keep their eye out for the killer whales.

What makes the open ocean so desolate? Mostly, it is the immense depth of the water. In shallow parts of the ocean, nutrients are recycled quickly. Materials sink down, but then currents, waves, and storms bring them back up again. But here, the water is just too deep. Nutrients that sink are lost from the food chain virtually forever.

Without nutrients, algae and plankton do not grow. And without algae and plankton, larger creatures cannot flourish. It should be noted that green plant life can only grow where there is sunlight. While a significant amount of light does penetrate the first 164 feet (50 m) of the open ocean, the remaining 12,836 feet (3,914 m) are shrouded in darkness and can only support certain life forms. This darkness does provide a temporary hiding place for both predator and prey, but many of these creatures must eventually return to the light.

At least twenty of the twenty-seven oceanic dolphins spend some of their time in the open ocean. What do they find there? A sparse layer of algae grows in the sunlit, topmost reaches of most open-ocean habitats. This plant growth is rich enough to attract a mixed group of larger creatures—fish, crustaceans, and squid—that in turn serve as prey for dolphins and other predators. But during the early daylight hours this mixed prey stays in the dark depths below the reach of the dolphins, only to rise toward the end of the day to the algae-rich upper levels under cover of the approaching darkness.

Many dolphin species, including spinner dolphins and Atlantic spotted dolphins, take advantage of this daily migration—diving to reach the shrimp, squid, flying fish, and other prey species rising toward the surface late in the day. These dolphin species hunt as long as they can, but they are largely visual hunters, and as the light fails their ability to catch prey decreases.

Spinner dolphins are a highly social species that typically swim together in large formations in the open ocean. Other open-ocean dolphins that swim in formation include Atlantic spotted

THE DEEPER PARTS OF
THE OCEAN ARE LIKE
VAST DESERTS, CON-
TAINING VERY FEW
LIVING THINGS.

dolphins, common dolphins, Fraser's dolphins, pantropical spotted dolphins, and striped dolphins. Why do these dolphins band together? Like zebra and wildebeest on the African plain, dolphins stay in plain view of their enemies—sharks and killer whales—during every moment of the day. On its own, a lone dolphin is open to attack. As a member of a group, a dolphin becomes part of a thing much larger than itself. In fact, the larger the group, the greater each individual's chance of survival becomes.

Open-ocean dolphins tend to have much brighter colors and bolder patterns than coastal or river dolphins. These features

ALMOST ALL DOLPHINS ARE SOCIAL CREATURES. THIS DOLPHIN SEEMS TO BE SMILING INTO THE AQUARIUM, WHERE PEOPLE HAVE COME TO VISIT.

help the group defend itself against predators. Dolphins in formation can respond to a threat at a speed faster than each individual is able to swim. A disturbance in the formation pattern of a school travels from one end of the group to the other almost instantaneously, allowing individual dolphins to alter their course before the threat gets near.

Why don't all dolphin species travel in large groups? They probably would if food sources allowed it. But though the open ocean is relatively lacking in prey compared to shore areas, the shore habitats have many more competitors (fish, reptiles, birds, and other mammals) for the same prey. More importantly, large schools of dolphins require large schools of prey species, and the open ocean is the only place where swarming schools of creatures are found.

Coastal Dolphins

Coastal regions are richer and more varied than the open ocean. Where the open ocean seems empty and monotonous, the coasts are teeming with life and energy. The coastal region begins at the edge of the continental shelf. On one side lies the shallow-water shelf; on the other side there is a sharp drop-off that leads to the near-freezing waters below.

This continental edge in many regions is a place that attracts dolphins. Prey species live near the edge because it is often a location of upwelling, where nutrient-rich waters from the ocean bottom return to the top. What causes this upwelling? Storms and other disturbances often displace waters in coastal regions. When these waters move out, other water must rush in to replace what has been removed. This replacement water ultimately must come from the nutrient-rich deep ocean, and its entry to shallower coastal waters takes place at the edge of the shelf.

COASTAL DOLPHINS TEND TO BE LESS SLEEK AND TRAVEL IN SMALLER GROUPS THAN DEEP-WATER OPEN-OCEAN SPECIES. FASTER-SWIMMING DOLPHINS TEND TO HAVE SMALLER FLUKES AND FINS.

The result of deep-water nutrients being brought to shallow waters is an explosion of growth. Plants, algae, and plankton along the edge attract fish, squid, and other prey animals, which in turn attract dolphins. Open-ocean dolphins such as spinners, Risso's dolphins, common dolphins, and striped dolphins often live along the continental edge. From the other direction, coastal species such as Atlantic white-sided dolphins, dusky dolphins, and white-beaked dolphins are also attracted to the edge habitat.

Coastal dolphins tend to be slower and squatter than open-ocean dolphins. Their bodies are more rounded, their flippers larger and more floppy, their eyesight less keen. Their body coloring is less bold and the schools they form are much smaller than the schools of open-ocean dolphins.

Each of these differences is rooted in where they live. In coastal regions, there are many more places for both prey and predators to hide. As one travels in from the continental edge, the waters become shallower, murkier, more full of nooks, crannies, and other hiding places, and more full of life. Coastal dolphins do not need speed or keen eyesight as much as they need maneuverability and knowledge about where prey is likely to

DOLPHINS FIND SAFETY IN NUMBERS BY TRAVELING IN GROUPS.

hide. They do not need to band together in huge schools for safety, so their body coloring does not need to be bright. In fact, many coastal dolphins, such as the bottlenose, the tucuxi, and the Atlantic hump-backed, are muted in color to blend in with their surroundings.

Though coastal dolphins never form schools numbering in the hundreds, they do form smaller schools that hunt and socialize together. Unlike the more rigid, formal, marching-band formations of open-ocean dolphins, the schools of coastal dolphins are flexible and fluid. Coastal dolphin schools form and re-form several times over a single day. This flexibility is perhaps what allows coastal dolphins to survive captivity so much better than open-ocean dolphins.

River Dolphin Habitats

Dolphins have been able to colonize only a few of the world's rivers, none of which is in North America. Rivers that do have dolphins living in them include the Yangtze in China, the Ganges and Brahmaputra in India, the Indus in Pakistan, and the Amazon-Orinoco system in South America.

In general, the characteristics of river dolphins reflect the habitats in which they live. Their underwater environment is often structured in a series of complex channels and passageways. Visibility in these habitats ranges from poor to nonexistent. Indeed, the susu, which lives in India, is commonly known as the blind dolphin because its eyesight is so poor. The susu, like other river dolphins, depends instead on its sense of touch and echolocation to navigate through its river home.

The habitats of river dolphins are even less wide-open than coastal habitats. River water is often shallow and muddy. Nooks, crannies, and hiding places abound. Rocks, boats, docks, islands,

RIVER DOLPHINS HAVE LITTLE USE FOR SHARP EYES BECAUSE THEY SPEND MOST OF THEIR TIME IN MURKY WATERS.

currents, wreckage, and plant life can crop up at any location. River dolphins have developed a number of adaptations well suited to this mazelike, unpredictable habitat. Their soft bodies are flexible, and their color is pale or muddy. They have small eyes, big, floppy fins, movable necks, and long beaks with as many as 200 razor-sharp teeth.

Because they live in such a murky environment, echolocation is critically important for river dolphins. Maneuverability is also key. River dolphins are the only dolphins that swim upside down. They can turn and twist in the water like contortionists. They use their sense of touch, as well as echolocation, to find their way through a river channel.

Because river dolphins live in such close proximity to people, they are especially vulnerable to water pollution, noise pollution, habitat destruction, boat collisions, and other disturbances caused by people. Several of the world's river dolphins are endangered species, including the Yangtze River baiji, the Indus River susu, and the Ganges River bhulan. The baiji population numbers fewer than one hundred and it may soon become extinct. Contrast this with coastal and open-ocean dolphins, of which only Hector's dolphin, with a population of nearly 4,000, is endangered.

4 Dolphins Up Close

There are twenty-seven oceanic dolphins, five river dolphins, and five porpoise species. In this chapter, you will get to know some of these species. Keep in mind that the boundaries between one dolphin species and another are sometimes blurred. Differences between the same dolphin species in two different habitats, or two different parts of the world, sometimes causes observers to split a species, such as the bottlenose dolphin or the common dolphin, into two or more species. Though the boundaries between dolphin species may change in the future, the species described in this chapter reflect a current classification based on body structure, molecular DNA, and cellular studies.

DOLPHINS ARE NATURAL-BORN ENTERTAINERS.

Spinner Dolphin, *Stenella longirostris*

Habitat: Open ocean
Beak: Prominent
Length: 5.5–7 feet (1.7–2.4 m)

These high-flying crowd-pleasers get their name from their spectacular spinning leaps. Spinners spin like Olympic figure skaters as they burst into the air at high speeds. Other than their close cousins, clymene dolphins, spinners are the only dolphins known to twist or spin as they leap. Spinners are also some of the most acrobatic and active dolphins. On a good leap, a spinner may make as many as four complete turns before it hits the water.

SPINNER DOLPHINS CAN TRAVEL IN HUGE GROUPS. WHEN HUNTING, A GROUP OF SPINNERS CAN STRETCH FOR MILES ACROSS.

Spinners are open-water dolphins that travel in groups ranging in number from a handful to a thousand or more. Spinner dolphins can be recognized by their long, thin beaks, slender bodies, and pointed flippers. Spinners will approach boats and hitch bow or wake rides for a half an hour or more, perhaps longer than any other dolphin. Years ago, spinners were sought out by aquarium owners who thought their acrobatic skills would work well in dolphin shows. Spinners, however, like most open-ocean species, do not do well in captivity.

Spinners associate with other schooling predators, including pantropical spotted dolphins and tuna. Because of their closeness to tuna schools, spinners have fallen victim to fishing nets, and their populations have decreased sharply.

Pantropical Spotted Dolphin, *Stenella attenuata*

Habitat: Open ocean and coast
Beak: Prominent
Length: 6–8.5 feet (1.9–2.6 m)

Not surprisingly, spots are the defining characteristic of pantropical spotted dolphins. Their light-colored, reflective spots shimmer in the sunlight as they glide alongside ships and boats, or bow ride or wake ride. Though almost all pantropical spotted dolphins have spots, the number and pattern of the spots varies with age and location. Older pantropical spotted dolphins sometimes have so many spots that the color beneath is not visible, while very young pantropicals have few if any spots.

Pantropical spotted dolphins are very active and playful at the water surface, but they are not as acrobatic as spinners. Typically, "spotters" make a series of low leaps followed by a higher breach as they completely separate from the water and land with a large splash. Pantropical spotted dolphins associate with other dolphin species, such as spinners, and with yellowfin tuna. Hundreds of thousands of pantropical spotted dolphins were lost in the decades before "dolphin-safe" tuna (tuna caught without harming dolphins) was introduced in 1994.

Atlantic Spotted Dolphin, *Stenella frontalis*

Habitat: Coast
Beak: Prominent
Length: 6.5–7.5 feet (2–2.3 m)

The Atlantic spotted dolphin is closely related to the pantropical spotted dolphin. The Atlantic spotted has a more narrow range—the mid-Atlantic—while the range of the pantropical spotted dolphin stretches in a wide band across the globe in tropical and temperate waters. The two spotted dolphins are not usually found together, though there are places in the Atlantic where they overlap. The Atlantic spotted dolphin is usually thicker than the pantropical spotted, has more spots, and is darker in color.

Dusky Dolphin, *Lagenorhynchus obscurus*

Habitat: Coast
Beak: Small
Length: 6–7 feet (1.9–2.2 m)

These small-beaked coastal dolphins are big on action, rivaled only by the spinners for putting on a show. Dusky dolphins are champion "breachers," leaping so high out of the water that they have been known to flip over completely. Like spinners, dusky dolphins love to travel beside boats and ships.

THE ATLANTIC SPOTTED DOLPHIN IS CLOSELY RELATED TO THE PANTROPICAL SPOTTED DOLPHIN. BOTH ARE CALLED SPOTTERS, AND BOTH OFTEN SPEND TIME WITH OTHER DOLPHINS.

Duskies live only in the Southern Hemisphere along the coasts of South America, southern Africa, and New Zealand. They are coastal dolphins, but stay in deeper coastal waters right up to the continental shelf. Duskies are among the best-studied dolphins in the world. Researchers along the coast of Argentina found that the same animals appear in the same regions year after year.

Behavioral studies of dusky dolphins have recognized three types of leap. When searching for a school of anchovies or other prey fish, the dolphins make silent, splashless, head-first leaps, presumably—not to disturb the prey while looking for

WHEN SEARCHING FOR PREY SUCH AS ANCHOVIES, DUSKY DOLPHINS MAKE SILENT, HEAD-FIRST LEAPS TO ENSURE SUCCESS IN THEIR MISSION.

seabirds—the clue that prey is nearby. Once the anchovies are spotted, the leap becomes more spectacular as the dolphins land on their backs or sides to make as big a splash as possible, perhaps to intimidate the prey into a tight formation.

A third type of leap occurs after feeding is over. Then, dusky dolphins leap high into the air and twist their bodies out of what appears to be sheer joy and exuberance, and land in the water in a great splash.

Risso's Dolphin, *Grampus griseus*

Habitat: Open ocean and Coast
Beak: Small
Length: 8.5–12 feet (2.6–3.7 m)

The large Risso's dolphin is sometimes classified as a blackfish, though usually it is put in the dolphin group. Risso's dolphin swims in almost every tropical and temperate ocean water on Earth, from coastlines to open oceans, from Iceland in the north to the tip of South America to the south.

Risso's dolphins are typically found in groups of fourteen or less. But in open-ocean areas, much larger groups have been reported, numbering perhaps in the thousands. Risso's look more like whales than other dolphins, and feed on squid, as does the sperm whale. Most Risso's are easy to identify. They have a blunt head, and, when mature, they are white and riddled with scars, perhaps from doing battle with squid.

The Risso's dolphin is also known as the gray grampus. Risso's genus name, *grampus*, originated from the French *grande poisson*, or very large "fish." In behavior, Risso's can be playful and frisky, often sitting up on the water with its head up, before turning and diving into the depths.

Atlantic White-Sided Dolphin, Lagenorhynchus acutus

Habitat: Open ocean and Coast
Beak: Small
Length: 7–9 feet (2.1–2.7 m)

The Atlantic white-sided dolphin is easy to recognize. Just look for the streak of yellow along the dolphin's rear flank. Atlantic white-sideds often share the water with the white-beaked dolphin (*Lagenorhynchus albirostris*) in the north Atlantic. Both species are members of the "lag" (*Lagenorhynchus*) dolphin group, which includes the dusky dolphin, the hourglass dolphin, and a few others. Atlantic white-sided dolphins resemble dusky dolphins in behavior. Both species are active and social, and both species spend most of their time along the continental shelf. Members of the lag group have the thickest blubber layers of any dolphin.

Pacific White-Sided Dolphin, *Lagenorhynchus obliquidens*

Habitat: Open ocean
Beak: Small
Length: 6.5 feet (2.0 m)

The Pacific white-sided dolphin may be the most people-friendly lag of all. Like other lags, the Pacific white-sided bow ride and wake ride and will perform a series of high-flying dives and stunts, including coordinated somersault jumps in groups of two or more. Pacific white-sideds swim with other cetacean species, including whales.

THE PACIFIC WHITE-SIDED DOLPHIN LOOKS MUCH LIKE A DUSKY DOLPHIN, BUT SWIMS IN THE NORTHERN RATHER THAN THE SOUTHERN HEMISPHERE, ALONG THE NORTH AMERICAN COAST TO ALASKA AND ALL THE WAY TO JAPAN.

Bottlenose Dolphin, *Tursiops truncatus*

Habitat: Open ocean and Coast
Beak: Long
Length: 7.5–12 feet (2.3–3.7 m)

The bottlenose dolphin is perhaps the world's best-known dolphin. When someone says "dolphin," the image of the bottlenose comes to mind. Bottlenoses are famous for a variety of reasons. First, the stars of the television show *Flipper* and of aquarium shows are often bottlenoses. Second, due to their friendly and curious nature, the "local legend" dolphins, such as Fungie, have been bottlenoses. Third, bottlenose dolphins, probably due to their closeness to human habitats, are by far the most well-studied dolphins in the world. Randall S. Wells and his partners in western Florida have carried out extensive studies on bottlenose dolphins.

One reason bottlenose dolphins are well known is that they are so widespread and easy to observe. Bottlenose dolphins appear in both coastal and open-ocean waters around the central latitudes of the world from below New Zealand in the south to the high latitudes of Greenland in the North Atlantic. They can adapt to almost any ocean environment. Some bottlenoses live in the open oceans. Others live close to the shore, even venturing up large river mouths at times. Still other bottlenose dolphins follow fishing boats and feed off the refuse they dump.

The bottlenose dolphins in each locality are a little bit different from other bottlenoses in both behavior and appearance. Many observers have proposed that not one but several different species make up the single dolphin species commonly called "bottlenose." So far, most experts feel that breaking up bottlenoses into subspecies or completely different species is unnecessary.

The hallmark of the bottlenose is its ability to adapt to local conditions. High-seas bottlenoses will have different behavior patterns from those that live close to shore. Yet, almost all bottlenoses seem to be playful, curious, and highly active. Indeed, such crowd-pleasers as Fungie became known because they approached boats first. It was their curiosity that bridged the gap between dolphin and human.

These bottlenose dolphins seem to leap for the pure joy of it.

Common Dolphin, *Delphinus delphis*

Habitat: Open ocean and Coast
Beak: Long
Length: 5.5–8 feet (1.7–2.4 m)

Confusion reigns when it comes to common dolphins. Not only are they frequently misidentified as spinner dolphins and Atlantic white-sided dolphins, but there are many kinds of common dolphins. Some observers have proposed splitting the animals now called common dolphins into several species. For now, however,

LIKE THE BOTTLENOSE AND A FEW OTHER SPECIES, LOCAL POPULATIONS OF COMMON DOLPHINS SEEM TO SHOW KEY DIFFERENCES. SOME CLASSIFICATION SCHEMES SPLIT COMMON DOLPHINS INTO MORE THAN ONE GROUP.

it appears that all common dolphins are local variations of two groups—the long-beaked and short-beaked common dolphin. These groups are widely distributed along the middle latitudes of all oceans, making the name "common dolphin" quite fitting for this species.

Common dolphins can be recognized from the hourglass pattern that covers their flanks and features a bright yellow or tan patch in front. Common dolphins are noisy creatures, often filling the air with high-pitched squeals and chirps as they surface in small groups. Common dolphins are active "porpoisers," or jumpers, performing a variety of tail-slaps, lob-tails, jumps, leaps, and other moves. Common dolphins feed at regular times each day, hunting for anchovies and other prey fish for about an hour, then breaking off for more playful, recreational swimming activities.

Harbor Porpoise, *Phocoena phocoena*

Habitat: Coast
Beak: Small
Length: 6 feet (1.8 m)

The harbor porpoise is small for a cetacean, shy, and not very friendly or curious about people. While dolphins often like to show off, porpoises typically keep to themselves and are sometimes seen resting at the surface.

The harbor porpoise and other members of the Phocoena family rarely jump, or breach. For the most part, they stay under the water and out of sight.

Harbor porpoises are in-shore animals, staying close to the coastline or in river mouths. Unlike dolphins, harbor porpoises tend to avoid boats and ships.

Boto, *Inia geoffrensis*

Habitat: River
Beak: Very long
Length: 5–9 feet (1.5–2.7 m)

The so-called pink porpoise is a dolphin that lives in the Amazon and Orinoco Rivers of South America. River dolphins are quite different from open-ocean or coastal dolphins. Where oceanic dolphins seem to be built for speed, river dolphins are a much slower and more cautious group. The rivers they inhabit are usually muddy and murky. Visibility is limited. So botos and other river dolphins navigate using echolocation rather than eyesight. Their eyes are small and not very keen. Botos' plump bodies seem soft and pliable. Unlike oceanic dolphins, they have flexible necks that can swivel and help them make sharper, more maneuverable turns than any of their ocean-dwelling relatives.

The boto has a long, thin snout, with as many as 132 sharp teeth for rooting through the muddy, plant-filled river bottom for fish, crustaceans, and other prey. Like other river species, the boto has a low dorsal fin and has the ability to swim upside down or backward. Though mature botos are generally pink, some botos are bluish gray or white.

Botos travel alone or with a single companion. In rare cases, as many as fifteen botos have been seen together in their South American river homes. Botos are the most numerous and widely distributed of all river dolphins. They share their habitats with the smaller tucuxi. The tucuxi dolphin can be found in two populations. The oceanic population lives along the coast of South America. The riverine population lives in the muddy Amazon, hundreds of miles upriver from the mouth.

THE BOTO'S LARGE, FLOPPY FLIPPERS ALLOW IT TO MANEUVER IN TIGHT CIRCLES AND SWIM IN ALL DIRECTIONS.

5 Dolphins in Action

Dolphins live in a highly competitive world. They compete not only within their own groups, but also with other dolphin species, as well as nondolphin species, such as sharks and tuna. With so many different kinds of rivals, it is natural to wonder, how can dolphins compete? After all, aren't dolphins, as mammals, at a disadvantage with respect to tuna, sharks, swordfish, and other large fish because of their need to surface for air every few minutes? How can dolphins effectively contend for prey and escape from predators with such a requirement?

Though it would appear that they might lose out to their nonmammal competitors, dolphins have several abilities and traits that give them a distinct edge. These include vertical swimming ability, high metabolism, superior sensory systems, and high intelligence. The intelligence of dolphins, in turn, appears to be responsible for their rich communication abilities—skills that perhaps give dolphins their greatest edge of all.

THE INTELLIGENCE OF DOLPHINS, AND MANY OF THEIR PHYSICAL CHARACTERISTICS, GIVE THESE CREATURES AN EDGE.

Vertical Swimming Ability

Though dolphins are no swifter or better able to maneuver than fish, their swimming style gives them an advantage in that it allows them to change depth quickly. Bony fish are equipped with an air sac inside their bodies that helps them maintain a steady depth without expending much energy. However, in an emergency, the air sac prevents them from changing depth quickly.

How does the dolphin's vertical ability translate into a competitive advantage? In some cases, dolphins can elude predators simply by going up or down. Perhaps more importantly, with the ability to change depth, dolphins can gain access to a range of food sources. Most fish are pretty much confined to a single general swimming depth, temperature, and location. Dolphins, on the other hand, can dive down and enter new habitats and environments that are unavailable to their competitors.

High Metabolism

The second advantage dolphins have over their cold-blooded rivals is high metabolism. Metabolism is the speed at which one's body "engine" runs. Cold-blooded (ectothermic) animals, such as fish and reptiles, have a relatively low metabolism. They do not create much body heat themselves but instead rely on the outside environment to warm their body to a high enough temperature to function efficiently.

Warm-blooded (endothermic) animals like dolphins make their own body heat. Rather than get warmth from the outer environment, endothermic animals burn fuel (food) to keep their bodies at a high temperature. Dolphins maintain their internal temperature at 98 degrees Fahrenheit (37°C)—about the same inner temperature that humans have. This high temperature

BOTTLENOSE DOLPHINS STAY CLOSE TO ONE ANOTHER. UNLIKE MANY OTHER CETACEANS, MOST DOLPHINS HAVE KEEN EYESIGHT AND CAN KEEP TRACK OF ONE ANOTHER VISUALLY AS WELL AS THROUGH SOUND, TOUCH, AND ECHOLOCATION.

allows dolphins to have a large, complex, high-performance brain. It enables dolphins to move at high speeds for long periods of time.

Though having a high metabolism helps dolphins outperform their cold-blooded rivals, it does not come without a cost. Dolphins have to burn more fuel to keep a high body temperature.

This is necessary because their large brains require a steady source of oxygen and glucose (blood sugar). In some respects, a warm-blooded animal is like a house with the heat on at all times. Keeping the inside warm makes the dolphin comfortable in cold waters but dolphins must eat more frequently than their cold-blooded competitors to stay warm and healthy. It is the price they pay for an important advantage.

Sensory Systems

A direct benefit of the dolphin's high metabolism is a set of efficient, specialized sensory systems. The dolphin's eyesight is greatly superior to the vision of most fish. The dolphin's sense of touch and hearing are also excellent, but it is echolocation that sets the dolphin apart from almost all of its rivals. Using echolocation, dolphins can locate prey more than 500 feet (152.4 m) away, see and navigate in complete darkness, and determine whether distant objects are hollow or solid.

Echolocation is based on the same principle as sonar. Using a structure deep inside the head, dolphins send out a series of clicks under water. They then gauge how far away an object is by how long it takes the echo to return.

How accurate and reliable is echolocation? Experiments have shown that dolphins in a tank can maneuver through a variety of obstacles and barriers while blindfolded. Other studies have shown that dolphins can distinguish and locate small objects using echolocation alone.

Echolocation gives dolphins an advantage that sharks, tuna, swordfish, and other big creatures of the deep cannot match. Though all dolphins have echolocation, most oceanic species, such as the pantropical spotted dolphin, rely on their vision to detect prey.

EVEN BLINDFOLDED, THIS BOTTLENOSE USES ECHOLOCATION TO CATCH THE RING. DOLPHINS HAVE NO PROBLEM LOCATING OBJECTS SMALLER THAN A DIME WITH THIS TECHNIQUE.

High Intelligence

Clearly, intelligence gives dolphins an advantage over competitors. And there is little doubt that dolphins are highly intelligent, especially when compared to sharks or tuna. Working with trainers, dolphins perform a wide variety of complex tricks, stunts, jumps, spins, and demonstrations. Dolphins can mimic; they have an excellent memory; they have learned to respond to human language; and scientists suspect that they possess a communication system of their own.

In laboratory experiments, dolphins have shown the ability to solve problems, show reasoning skills, and make "deals" with others. Dolphins are the only organism besides humans and great apes to recognize themselves in the mirror. In the military, some 240 dolphins have been trained by the U.S. Navy since 1960 to perform dangerous and technical tasks with great success. In the wild, dolphins show complex social behavior.

THE TRICKS THAT CAPTIVE DOLPHINS ARE ABLE TO PERFORM MAY ONLY SCRATCH THE SURFACE AT REVEALING THEIR TRUE INTELLIGENCE.

Their cooperative behavior helps them elude predators, protect their young, and herd prey so that it can be easily snapped up by the group.

Dolphins' intelligence includes the ability to identify individuals, dolphin and human, by sound and by sight. Dolphins are curious, helpful, and seem to be good-natured. Trainers often marvel at dolphins' ability to understand their body language and the spinning, diving, and nuzzling of other dolphins. Trainers also report a playfulness and a sense of humor in dolphins that seems unusual in the animal world.

The purpose of dolphin intelligence, however, may not be to defeat enemies but to get along socially within the dolphin group. Getting along in a complicated social system takes a lot of mental flexibility. Dolphins, like human beings, live complex lives that involve multiple relationships with many other individuals. Interpreting sounds, actions, body language, and other subtle signals from a variety of individuals in a constantly changing social environment requires a great deal of brain power.

PLAYING TOGETHER IS AN IMPORTANT PART OF BEING A POD MEMBER. NOTICE THAT THE YOUNG SPOTTED DOLPHINS DO NOT HAVE SPOTS YET.

Communication

There is no question that dolphins communicate. Anyone who has worked with dolphins knows how well they communicate nonverbally, picking up on gestures, body language, tone of voice, and other unspoken cues. People who have spent time with dolphins also have no doubt that dolphin "speech" is rich with rhythm, musical tone, and complexity. Indeed, dolphins are a race of chattering creatures, filling the air (and the water) with their clicks, whistles, chirps, pops, and a dozen other indescribable sounds.

The most pressing question about dolphin communication is not whether dolphins vocalize. Rather, the question is whether dolphin sounds form a language that makes sense, a language in which individual words and phrases have universal meanings that can be transferred from one situation to the next and that can be arranged and rearranged according to rules.

For example, dolphins have their own signature whistle. This distinctive sound is an example of a type of vocal communication. Dolphins use their signature whistle to announce their arrival on the scene to pod-mates. Many think of these whistles as being "like" names. When the pod-mates hear the whistle, they answer back, often mimicking the sound of the newcomer's signature whistle.

But many researchers do not believe that signature whistles qualify as language. In any case, signature whistles represent only one small part of the language puzzle. What researchers have discovered is that the various types of dolphin sounds can be separated into categories. Clicks make up one category. They are not a form of communication—they are reserved for echolocation. Whistles, squawks, blats, and moans may carry information, but no one is sure. So the question of whether

CONVEYING INFORMATION BY MOVEMENT AND GESTURE IS A NATURAL FORM OF COMMUNICATION FOR A DOLPHIN.

dolphins speak a true language remains to be solved.

Perhaps dolphins really communicate best nonverbally. Many dolphin researchers speculate that dolphins use movement and touch to communicate a wealth of information about mood, emotion, and even ideas. For example, after a successful foray into the deep for fish, a returning dolphin might use a series of leaps, spins, and gestures to communicate the direction and depth at which the prey could be found. Additional information could be communicated through touch. However, little evidence supports the existence of a formal nonverbal language. If dolphins do use a nonverbal language, researchers have not been able to translate it into a form that humans can understand and appreciate.

6 The Life of a Dolphin

However they learn to communicate, dolphins, as do other species, must be born, and that process begins with courtship and mating.

Courtship and Mating

At best, researchers have a sketchy knowledge of courtship and mating behavior for most dolphin species. Most of what is known describes the behavior of bottlenose dolphins, who are by far the best-studied dolphin species. Maturity for female bottlenose dolphins takes place between ages five and twelve. For males, sexual maturity occurs between ages nine and fourteen. At this time young males leave their mothers' pods to join roving bands of other young males.

Young bottlenose males swim and hunt together, gaining confidence in themselves until they are ready to approach a female. Generally, relationships within the male group evolve over

VERY LITTLE IS KNOWN ABOUT DOLPHIN COURTSHIP. MOST OF THE RESEARCH HAS BEEN DONE ON BOTTLENOSE DOLPHINS, SUCH AS THIS ONE.

time. Each male struggles for dominance—fighting, chasing, and pushing the others as he tries to become the group's alpha male.

Eventually, the group will corral a female member of a pod and attempt to mate with her. Behavior at this point can get heated. Rival males may attempt to steal away the male's hard-earned female. The female seems to accept the male only reluctantly, often biting and snapping at him, as if to make him prove every step of the way that he is ready, able, and dominant. Generally, the more mature and dominant the male, the less he is challenged by other males—or females—for the right to mate. When a male and female do get together, they mate belly to belly. Pregnancy is quite long in most dolphin species. While bottlenose dolphins take about twelve months to give birth, evidence suggests that other dolphin species take even longer.

Birth

Finally, the twelve months have passed and the female bottlenose dolphin gives birth to her calf. The 44 pound (20 kg) baby comes out of the birth canal tail first, attached to the umbilical cord, surprisingly large and well formed. After the cord breaks, the calf must sink or swim. To get its first breath of fresh air, the calf must rise to the surface.

After taking a breath, the young calf will stick close to its mother, following her every move, riding in her wake and below her. Dolphin calves tend to be among the largest of mammal newborns, probably due to the circumstances of their birth. While most other mammals can retreat to a cozy burrow or den to give birth, the dolphin's open-water home has no defined boundaries to protect the mother or calf.

Starting life in the open favors the birth of large, fully formed offspring that are ready for action as soon as they are

born. This readiness is put to the test immediately because blood in the water from the birth arouses a flurry of sharks to gather. The nervous calf will stick close to its mother as members of the entire pod come to its defense. Surrounding the mother and child like the defensive linemen on a football team, they successfully drive away the hostile intruders, leaving the baby to spend its first few moments in the world in peace.

With the sharks safely out of sight, the calf will proceed to get its first meal, the rich milk that comes out of the nipple on the lower side of the mother's abdomen. Dolphin milk is powerful stuff; it has ten times the food value of cow's milk. While wonderfully nutritious for the calf, such rich milk puts a great strain on the health of the mother. After several suckling sessions in which the milk is squirted under pressure directly into the baby's mouth, the mother is depleted and in need of nutrition herself.

Caring for Young Dolphins

The need to take time out to find food may indeed be a major reason why dolphins have come to be such social creatures. On her own, the young mother would probably never manage to raise her calf. The dangers would just be too great—sooner or later she would turn her back and the calf would be snatched up by a shark, killer whale, or some other enemy, or might become separated from its mother in a storm. But with the help of pod-mates, the job becomes more manageable. As social animals, dolphins look out for one another. So when the mother goes off hunting, others step in to protect the calf.

In many cases, new mothers recruit a permanent baby-sitter to help with the care of their offspring. This helper is typically a mature female pod-mate, perhaps a close relative, who currently has no young offspring herself. During the first few days after birth, the helper will be the only one that the mother lets get near to the calf. Together, the two, along with other female pod members, look after the calf until it is old enough to be on its own.

Male dolphins, however, take no role in the raising of offspring. They typically come from distant pods and disappear as soon as mating takes place. This, it turns out, is a good thing.

The problem with male dolphins (and many other mammal males) is not that they are selfish or lazy, but that they are likely to kill the offspring if they get too close.

In the animal world, the interest of both males and females is to further their own genes. Mothers have no worry about whether

THESE DOLPHINS FIND SAFETY IN NUMBERS. IN GENERAL, DEEP-WATER DOLPHINS FORM LARGER GROUPINGS THAN COASTAL SPECIES.

offspring are their own. But for fathers, the issue can be in doubt, especially if, as with dolphins, males and females do not form exclusive mating pairs. Since females mate with more than one male, males are often not sure who has sired the calf. It makes sense, then, for males to try to get rid of another's offspring to force the mother to start all over again, this time mating with him to make sure that the calf is his own.

This killing of offspring, known as infanticide, may sound unspeakably cruel and heartless, but human mating systems are largely exclusive, one-to-one relationships in which males have confidence that they are the fathers of offspring. With dolphins, paternity is always in doubt, so dolphin males express this uncertainty by not participating in the raising of offspring.

Safe with their mothers, young bottlenose dolphins grow up in the confines of the pod. A pod is a long-term social unit, something like a human family. Though pod structures of dolphin species vary, the best-studied pods are those of bottlenose dolphins. These pods have an average of seven members. The pods contain mother-calf pairs, youngsters of both sexes, and other adult females of various ages. They differ from human families in not including adult males.

Growing Up

Before they reach the age of maturity, male youngsters and teens spend time in their mothers' pods. The young preadolescent calves of both sexes grow up playing together, learning hunting and social skills much like the cubs of land animals such as lions or dogs. Within a pod, a hierarchy emerges in which pod members are ranked according to their status in the group. The leaders, or alphas, exercise control over the lesser-ranked animals by using nudges, gestures, and other forms of body language. The pod does everything together. At times, it may become part of a larger group, as individual pods join up to form superpods for hunting or other activities. But after the activity is over, individual pods split off to spend time on their own.

At adolescence, males break off into small buddy groups of two to three members. These groups are likely to be quite stable, with group members traveling and hunting together for years.

THE TYPICAL POD HAS ABOUT SEVEN MEMBERS, BUT DOLPHINS ARE CONSTANTLY FORMING AND RE-FORMING NEW GROUPS OF VARIOUS SIZES. HERE, THREE SPOTTED DOLPHINS SPEND TIME TOGETHER.

Sometimes males break off to be on their own. Battle can be heated between rival male groups as they fight for the right to escort and mate with females. These conflicts can be extremely fierce, resulting in injury to the loser or perhaps banishment from the pod. Among bottlenoses, the struggle for dominance between groups can stretch out over time, with power alliances forming, breaking up, and then re-forming as groups jockey to gain control.

SPINNER DOLPHINS DIVE TOGETHER.

Dolphins are social animals, but because they spend their time largely out of view of observers, researchers know little of the daily social interactions that take place within a dolphin pod. It is clear that the mother-child bond is the strongest and most durable relationship in the dolphin world. But friendships within male groups are also strong, and so are the relationships between females within a pod.

Daily life among oceanic dolphin species is apparently a fluid, yet structured experience. Studies of Florida dolphins show that they tend to repeat the same or similar activities each day. Groupings of pods form and re-form at different times during

UNLIKE LAND ANIMALS, DOLPHINS HAVE NO PHYSICAL HOME. TO A DOLPHIN, "HOME" IS WHEREVER POD-MATES ARE.

the day. A single pod may join others in feeding or some other activity, then break off on its own when the activity ends. Generally, the farther a group of dolphins is from the shore, the more time it spends in very large groupings. Thus spinner and Atlantic spotted dolphins often congregate in groups of several hundred for at least part of each day. Open-ocean bottlenose dolphins also gather in large groups, while bottlenoses that live in shallow coastal water spend more of their time in smaller groups. Coastal species that live in murky waters congregate in even smaller groups. The hump-backed dolphin and Irrawaddy, for example, never associate in groups larger than a few individuals.

Because each dolphin interacts with its own pod-mates as well as the members of other pods, the typical open-ocean dolphin carries on relationships with dozens, if not hundreds, of other dolphins. This social complexity, some scientists think, may be the reason behind why dolphins developed such large brains—they need high intelligence to keep track of all of their friends and enemies. Of course, if this explanation is true then you would expect the coastal dolphins that gather in smaller groups to be less intelligent. So far, this hypothesis has not been borne out.

As with social life, dolphin feeding behavior is influenced by grouping and habitat. Open-ocean dolphins usually feed on schooling fish, while coastal species tend to be specialist feeders that track individual fish, crustaceans, and other prey to their hiding places.

Cooperative behavior has been frequently observed in several dolphin species. Oceanic bottlenose dolphins and dusky dolphins have been seen encircling a school of fish, then herding them into a tight ball, only to let individual dolphins swim to the center of the circle and take turns capturing prey. Other dolphin species that live closer to shore have also been known to work together to push schools of fish onto a shallow sandbar where they can easily be snapped up. Dolphins eat prey whole without chewing. For extremely large prey, a dolphin might stun its victim first with a tail slap, then move in to take its dazed victim.

Dolphin social life is not restricted to interactions with other dolphins. Some dolphin species also exhibit a type of social behavior with yellowfin tuna. Pantropical spotted dolphins and other dolphin species swim in large groups in the same area as yellowfin tuna. The mingling typically takes place in the open ocean surrounding large bits of debris, such as broken logs. There, groups of dolphins swim with large schools of tuna, apparently attracted by the floating debris. How do the dolphins benefit from swimming amidst hundreds of hungry predators that are hunting the same prey?

Researchers are not sure what the attraction is. Perhaps the tuna act as a decoy, drawing sharks and other enemies away from the dolphins as they hunt for prey. Or perhaps it is the tuna that are following the dolphins, benefiting from their prey-finding abilities.

While dolphins in captivity have lived as long as fifty years, in the wild various dangers limit dolphin life spans to about twenty years. Many dolphins suffer from parasite infestations of one type or another. Nematode (small worms) infections of the lungs cause dolphins to wheeze from their blowholes. Other infections from bacteria, fungi, and larger parasites, such as lampreys, also plague dolphins and cut short their life spans.

Predators also threaten dolphins. Sometimes disease and predators go hand in hand. A sick dolphin that cannot keep up with the group is often attacked by a shark or killer whale. Predators also take advantage of the other two times in a dolphin's life when it is most vulnerable—just after it is born and when a young adult is going off on its own to join a new pod. In general, predators are most successful in hunting dolphins that are sick, injured, or distressed in some way. Healthy adult dolphins that belong to cohesive pods are rarely victims of predators.

Perhaps the strangest occurrence that reduces dolphin populations is the phenomenon of strandings. Strandings are horrifying sights to a dolphin lover. A single dolphin, or perhaps a group, will be found beached on the sand, unable or unwilling to get back into the water. Strandings are fairly common. On some shallow beaches that have large tidal changes, strandings

STRANDINGS ARE AS MUCH A MYSTERY AS THEY ARE A TRAGEDY. EXPOSURE TO THE SUN IS A SERIOUS DANGER TO ANIMALS THAT LIVE UNDERWATER.

occur quite regularly, suggesting that there is something about these kinds of locations that pose a particular danger to dolphins.

Stranded animals can sometimes be helped back to the safety of the water. But in most cases, stranding victims die on the beach, crushed under their own weight without the support of water. The cause of strandings is a mystery. Are strandings, as some observers suggest, a form of suicide? Other theories to account for the cause of strandings include magnetic navigation disturbances, inner ear parasites, and confusion from noise pollution. Whatever the cause of stranding, the result takes its toll—thousands of dolphins are victims of strandings every year.

Perhaps the most important factors in the reduction of dolphin populations come from interactions with people. Getting trapped in tuna nets is the greatest danger to dolphins. But other hazards are created either directly or indirectly by humans. These hazards include water pollution, boat collisions, hunting, and habitat loss.

7 Dolphins, Today and Tomorrow

If only dolphins could swim backward. Then, when they accidentally got stuck in commercial fishing nets, they could just back up and find a way to escape. But once most oceanic dolphins swim into a net, they find themselves with only one option—to keep on churning ahead, and they eventually end up hopelessly entangled.

The situation is both tragic and ironic. It is tragic because no one wants to kill dolphins. There is no market for dolphin meat, and the fishing industry has no interest in hunting dolphins directly. Dolphins end up getting trapped unintentionally in fishing nets.

The situation is ironic because, as animals that spend their entire lives in the water, it would seem as though drowning would be the last thing dolphins would need to worry about. But dolphins are mammals, not fish, and mammals need to return to the surface every few minutes to replenish their oxygen supply.

DRIFT NETS CONTINUE TO PRESENT A MAJOR DANGER TO DOLPHINS. THE MOST IMPORTANT ALLY DOLPHINS HAVE IS PUBLIC OPINION.

The introduction of gigantic drift nets to catch swordfish and other commercial fish species in the 1960s spelled disaster for many oceanic dolphin species. These nets, often measuring 30 miles (48 km) in length, were put out to sea each evening, trapping anything and everything in their path, including sea turtles, birds, sharks, cephalopods (squid and octopuses), and blackfish. Made of thin nylon, the nets were largely undetectable by echolocation—so dolphins had little means of avoiding them.

So many dolphins were being trapped in drift nets during the 1970s and 1980s that in 1992 the United Nations instituted a ban on nets any greater than 1.6 miles (2.6 km) in length. This improved the situation somewhat. But then dolphins were caught in the newer, smaller gill nets. They were attracted to the fish and other prey creatures caught in the nets and became trapped themselves.

Perhaps an even worse situation developed in the tuna-fishing industry. Here, the net of choice was the baglike purse-seine net, which closed around its prey like a cinched laundry sack. These nets would probably not have caused any great hazard for cetaceans were it not for the habit of several dolphin species to swim with yellowfin tuna. In many open-ocean waters, the two are almost inseparable. Wherever you find dolphins, you find yellowfins swimming below.

Why this dolphin-tuna bond exists is a mystery. Do the dolphins help the tuna, or is it the other way around? Or do the two somehow help each other find prey or protect themselves from predators?

Whatever reason dolphins have for swimming with yellowfins, one fact is certain: fishing boats use dolphins to find yellowfins. The process is called "setting on the dolphins." Rather than search directly for yellowfins, fishing boats look for dolphins instead. Once they locate the dolphins they cast their nets, confident that they will find yellowfins swimming beneath.

By the early 1970s as many as 500,000 dolphins were being killed each year by purse-seine tuna fishing. Something had to be done. By 1990, new rules were put into place to create "dolphin-safe" tuna. These rules have reduced the number of dolphins killed to perhaps 5,000 or less per year. The situation has improved, but too many dolphins are still being lost needlessly each year.

THE TUNA INDUSTRY HAS GREATLY REDUCED THE NUMBER OF DOLPHINS TAKEN, BUT MANY THOUSANDS ARE STILL KILLED EACH YEAR.

How can dolphin drownings be eliminated in the fishing industry? Several ideas to cut down on dolphin losses have been tried. Many fishing boats now cast nets with escape hatches—doors or holes in the nets that allow dolphins to escape. These measures can be moderately successful if the fishing boats monitor their nets closely. But close monitoring takes time and many worker hours. For a fishing boat to hire a "dolphin observer" to make sure that dolphins are not trapped is a lot to ask—especially when you consider that this observer does not help increase the boat's catch by a single fish.

A second idea for eliminating dolphin losses is to place electronic beeping devices on fishing nets. These electronic pingers serve two purposes. First, they warn dolphins away from deadly nets, and second, they scare them from ever coming near in the first place.

Do pingers work? The results are mixed. Some experiments have shown that pingers can be successful in the short term. But over the long term, pingers may create as many problems as they solve. Once dolphins get used to the electronic noises they may learn to ignore them. More importantly, dolphins may actually become attracted to the pingers, once they learn to associate the electronic sound with the prey animals typically caught in the nets in which the pinger is installed.

Overall, great improvements have been made in eliminating dolphin losses from fishing, but far too many open-ocean dolphins are still being killed each year.

In-Shore Threats

In many ways, the dangers faced by open-ocean dolphins are different from those faced by coastal dolphin populations. Problems faced by open-ocean dolphins come primarily from the fishing industry. The major problem facing coastal and river dolphins is pollution. Why doesn't pollution pose as great a threat to open-ocean habitats? The ocean beyond the continental shelf is just too vast and deep to show the serious effects of dumping, agricultural runoff, and other pollution sources that originate on land.

This is not the case for coastal and river dolphins. Pollutants in these shallow water habitats tend to accumulate, instead of getting washed away. Coastal and river dolphins face a variety of other environmental threats, including collisions with ships, boats, and personal watercraft, noise pollution from military sonar and other sources, algal bloom, sewage, pesticides, and

BECAUSE THEY ARE TOP PREDATORS THAT EAT SMALLER CREATURES, DOLPHINS INGEST POLLUTION IN ITS MOST CONCENTRATED FORM.

other forms of chemical and thermal pollution, as well as habitat loss from dredging, dams, river engineering, overfishing, and other causes.

Many of these problems could be corrected without too much hardship. Recreational boaters, for example, might learn to stay on the lookout for dolphins and their habitats and to slow down and take care when they get near. Shipping lanes for commercial freight haulers could be redrawn to minimize harm to dolphins. Some forms of noise pollution could also be reduced with intelligent and careful planning.

But most forms of pollution cannot be so easily corrected. Away from the shore, the ocean is so vast that most forms of pollution are dwarfed by its sheer size. But along shallow coastlines, pollutants build up and cannot be easily washed away. In and around bays and river mouths, where waters are shallow, irregular, and closed off, pollution problems become even more acute.

Sewage and other forms of dumping can poison dolphins where they live. Fortunately, these forms of pollution can be controlled in many cases. Sewage treatment plants can make coastal habitats safe for dolphins and other organisms. Dumping laws, if strictly enforced, can also eliminate many types of chemical and industrial pollution. More troublesome are agricultural runoffs, such as pesticides, fertilizers and animal waste, and toxic chemicals from manufacturing. Long-lasting poisons from these sources pose a danger to all ocean creatures, but the hazard they present to top predators like dolphins is especially harmful.

When long-lasting poisons like DDT and dieldren (both used to kill insects) and PCBs (chemicals used as coolants and lubricants) get into the food chain, they are hard to remove. They do not break down naturally like many other chemicals. Instead, the toxins collect and become concentrated as they move up through the food chain.

As mammals that breathe air, dolphins are some of the primary victims of this oil spill, which has spread over the surface of the water.

Tiny plankton make up the bottom of the food chain. Each plankton organism may take up a small quantity of toxin—a few thousand toxin particles, or units, for example—as they live and grow. Larger crustaceans and other small creatures eat the plankton, each collecting toxins from the thousands of individual plankton creatures that they ingest. From there, small fish and squid continue the collection process, taking in large numbers of crustaceans and other small creatures, each of which contains collected toxins. So, by the time the fish and squid are eaten by dolphins, millions of toxin units have collected in the bodies of their prey. Thus, dolphins are subjected to a more concentrated form of poison than the other creatures on the lower rungs of their food chains.

Though toxic chemicals are immensely destructive, their use is gradually being cut down in the environment as scientists and governments learn more about their deadly effects. This is not the case with the various fertilizers, chemicals, and other runoffs from farms, industry, and even suburban backyards that end up in the oceans. These substances wash into rivers, whose currents eventually carry them to places where dolphins live. While fertilizers do not poison sea animals directly, they often provide so much nutrition to waters that an immense algal bloom develops, becoming so dominant that it uses up the oxygen supply in the vicinity, killing off fish and other organisms and destroying dolphin habitats.

Dolphin habitats are also being destroyed by land development projects and overfishing. The building of shore communities and the hazards they present crowd dolphins out of riverine and coastal habitats. Overfishing presents a bigger threat, as human fishers haul in such large catches that fish are not able to replenish themselves. Without enough prey animals to survive, dolphin populations suffer.

The list of threats to dolphins goes on and on. Oil spills, deforestation pollution, damming, air pollution, coal mine waste, and many other hazards threaten dolphins in a variety of ways. Dolphin habitats are being lost every day. In China, the river dolphin known as the baiji, already down to dangerously low population levels, faces a new threat in the proposed Three Gorges Dam in the Yangtze River.

Threats to other river dolphins, the susu of India (5,000 estimated to be left), and the bhulan of Pakistan (500 estimated left), are also serious. Will the baiji, susu, and bhulan also become extinct? Many observers feel that river dolphins, inhabitants of shallow and vulnerable habitats, will not be able to survive the environmental pressures brought about by twenty-first century river development. Some marine species, such as the vaquita, or Gulf of California porpoise (fewer than 200 left), or the coastal Hector's dolphin (about 4,000 left) are also threatened. Will they too disappear? Again, only time will tell.

No doubt, it would be a tragedy if any dolphin species were to be lost. But is the extinction of dolphins more tragic than the disappearance of any one of thousands of other threatened species?

Dolphins are remarkable creatures. They are friendly and clearly intelligent. Dolphins exhibit complex behavior and have a rich social life. Their brains are larger, in proportion to body size, than most other animals. The mirror and ink spot experiments indicate that dolphins have a measure of self-awareness. They recognize themselves. Signature whistle studies suggest that dolphins may have unique identities that take on the form of names—a trait that, if proven, they share only with human beings.

All of these qualities are remarkable, but when you add them up what do they mean? After all, a variety of organisms

DOLPHINS IN CAPTIVITY HELP SCIENTISTS LEARN BETTER WAYS TO TREAT DOLPHINS IN
THE WILD.

exhibit many of the special traits that dolphins have. Dogs are
friendly and fairly intelligent. Bees possess a remarkable nonverbal communication system. Chimpanzees and other primates
seem to have more capacity to learn language than do dolphins.
Moreover, chimpanzees exhibit a greater sense of self-awareness

than do dolphins. And as far as brain structure—the size and organization of an animal's brain is by no means the final word on its intelligence. The spiny anteater, for example, seems to have a key brain structure (the neocortex) that is proportionally much larger than that of dolphins; indeed, the brain structure in spiny anteaters—in proportion to their body size—is even larger than that of humans.

It would seem that dolphins merit no more special status than countless other creatures. Accordingly, they should be given the same consideration as other animal species—no more and no less. And, in fact, this is the position most thoughtful scientists take. Dolphins are important to the whole environment and all its life forms. But so are many animals. We should worry about killing dolphins and losing dolphin habitats not so much because dolphins are unique and wonderful. More importantly, in an ecosystem, everything is connected. Harming one species inevitably harms another.

There is the possibility that dolphin intelligence and self-awareness go beyond a modest sense of self to, as some dolphin enthusiasts claim, a higher and more spiritual plane—a level of consciousness that equals or surpasses that of human beings. Are these claims true?

No one knows for sure.

It is possible that dolphins possess special healing powers, that they can use their echolocation skills to see through objects and situations that humans are not aware of, and that their large brains give them the ability to have advanced thoughts and communicate them through a complicated code that consists of body and sound language.

It is also possible that dolphins are no more advanced than dogs or house cats—a bit more intelligent, perhaps, but on the whole at the same level.

Both of these descriptions are possible. What's more likely is that dolphins fall somewhere in between the two extremes—they are more advanced than dogs, but certainly not the magical, intuitive, wondrous beings that some people believe they are.

Perhaps we should leave it at that. Dolphins are amazing and fascinating creatures worthy of our highest admiration. But rather than single out dolphins and put them on a pedestal where they enjoy star status, why not use our admiration for this remarkable group of animals to appreciate and celebrate how special, unique, and wonderful all animal species are? This may be the true lesson that dolphins teach us—that by understanding and valuing their extraordinary qualities we begin to gain a richer and deeper appreciation for all creatures, large and small.

Glossary

abyssal plain—flat ocean bottom with an average depth of 13,000 feet (4,000 m)

adaptation—a change in body form or function as a result of natural selection

alpha—leader, or dominant, dolphin

atmosphere—a unit of measure equal to the amount of air pressure at sea level; water pressure increases by 1 atmosphere for every 10 meters of depth

blackfish—a member of the family Delphinidae not usually considered a dolphin: killer whales, pilot whales, and others

blubber—body fat

bow ride—to ride on the wave created by the bow of a moving boat

breach—a jump out of the water by a dolphin or whale

cetacean—any member of the whale family, including baleen whales and toothed whales (dolphins are a special group of toothed whale)

continental shelf—the shallow ocean region that extends about 45 miles (72 km) out from a continent

Delphinidae—the family of cetaceans that includes oceanic dolphins and blackfish

DNA—deoxyribonucleic acid—the substance inside every cell that contains the genetic code; DNA is used to test how closely different animals species are related

drift net—giant nets (30 miles, or 48 km, in length) used to catch fish that were banned in the 1970s

echolocation—a system that uses sound and echoes to detect the environment

ectotherm—a cold-blooded animal that relies mainly on its environment for heat

endotherm—a warm-blooded animal that generates its own body heat

fluke—the horizontal tail of a cetacean

gill net—smaller nets that replaced drift nets in the ocean-fishing industry

habitat—the environment in which an animal species lives

intertidal zone—the ocean zone closest to land that is covered and uncovered by tides

infanticide—the killing of infant dolphins

mammals—animals that have hair, give milk, and give birth to live young; cetaceans and human beings are mammals

mesonychid condylarth—an ancestor of the cetaceans that lived about 53 million years ago and resembled a wolf

metabolism—the speed at which a body uses energy

morphology—body structure

mysticetes—baleen cetaceans

natural selection—the process of selecting for traits that increase the chances of an animal's survival

ondontocetes—toothed cetaceans

oxygen—a chemical element and gas that animals use to burn their food to get energy

parasite—an animal that lives by feeding on another living animal

pingers—electronic noisemakers designed to drive dolphins away from nets

plankton—any ocean life form that drifts rather than swims actively

pod—a social group of cetaceans that functions as a family

population—the number of animals of a given species in a given place

porpoise—the smallest cetaceans, including Dall's porpoise, harbor porpoise, and vaquita

predator—an animal that hunts and eats other animals for food

prey—an animal that is hunted for food

purse-seine net—a fishing net that closes around prey like a cinched sac

self-awareness—the state of knowing of one's existence; humans, chimpanzees, and dolphins are the only animals known to possess self-awareness

signature whistle—a call of dolphins, thought by some people to be a unique identifying name

species—a type of organism that is distinct and completely different from all other life forms

stranding—when a cetacean is left to die on the beach

upwelling—the rapid movement of bottom water to top water layers to replace water moved out by storms and other causes

wake ride—to ride on the wave created behind a moving boat

Species Checklist

The list below identifies some of the dolphin species living in the world today. Like all living things, dolphins are given both common and scientific names. Common names are usually written in lowercase, unless taken from a proper name. Scientific names, which are in Latin, should be italicized with the first, or genus, name capitalized and the second, which identifies the species, in lowercase.

Atlantic humpback	*Sousa teuszii*
Atlantic spotted	*Stenella frontalis*
Atlantic white-sided	*Lagenorhynchus acutus*
baiji	*Lipotes vexillifer*
bhulan	*Platanista minor*
boto	*Inia geoffrensis*
bottlenose	*Tursiops truncatus*
clymene	*Stenella clymene*
common	*Delphinus delphis*
Dall's porpoise	*Phocoenoides dalli*
dusky	*Lagenorhynchus obscurus*
finless porpoise	*Neophocaena phocaenoides*
franciscana	*Pontoporia blainvillei*
Fraser's	*Lagenodelphis hosei*
Harbor porpoise	*Phocoena phocoena*
Hector's	*Cephalorhynchus hectori*
hourglass	*Lagenorhynchus cruciger*
Irrawaddy	*Orcaella brevirostris*
killer whale	*Orcinus orca*
Pacific white-sided	*Lagenorhynchus obliquidens*
pantropical spotted	*Stenella attenuata*
Risso's	*Grampus griseus*
spectacled porpoise	*Australophocaena dioptrica*
spinner	*Stenella longirostris*
striped dolphin	*Stenella coeruleoalba*
susu	*Platanista gangetica*
tucuxi	*Sotalia fluviatilis*
vaquita	*Phocoena sinus*
white-beaked	*Lagenorhynchus albirostris*

Further Research

Here are some recommended resources for further research on dolphins.

Books for Young People

Barlowe, Sy. *Learning about Dolphins*. Mineola, NY: 2001.

Berger, Melvin, and Gilder Berger. *Is a Dolphin a Fish? Questions and Answers about Dolphins*. New York: Scholastic, Inc., 2001.

Byrun, Jody. *Dolphins and Porpoises: A World Beyond the Waves*. Orlando, FL: SeaWorld, Inc., 2000.

Kallen, Stuart A. *Dolphins and Porpoises*. Cambridge, MA: Gale Group, 2002.

Web Sites

http://www.cetacea.org/dolphins.htm
   A Web site with clickable buttons for each dolphin species.

http://www.irishdolphins.com
   A Web site that gives information on friendly wild dolphins, including Fungie.

http://animal.discovery.com/animal.html
   The search function on this site can be used to find the dolphin links and features.

http://www.highnorth.no/Library/Myths/br-be-an.htm
   A Web site that includes a 1994 article about dolphin intelligence by researcher and dolphin authority Margaret Klinowska.

http://home.snafu.de/ulisses/tursiops.htm
   An article by Ulrich Reinartz that discusses dolphin intelligence.

Bibliography

Baker, Mary L. *Whales, Dolphins, and Porpoises of the World*. Garden City, NY: Doubleday, 1987.

Benton, Major, and Susan Yoder. *The Wisdom of Dolphins*. Naperville, IL: Sourcebooks, Inc., 2000.

Bright, Michael. *Dolphins*. New York: Gallery Books, 1985.

Carwardine, Mark. *Whales, Dolphins, and Porpoises*. London: Dorling Kindersley, 1995.

Carwardine, Mark R., Ewan Fordyce, Peter Gill, and Erich Hoyt. *Whales, Dolphins, and Porpoises*. New York: Dorling Kindersley, 1998.

Kerrod, Robin. *Whales and Dolphins*. London: Lorenz Books, 1998.

May, John, ed., *The Greenpeace Book of Dolphins*. New York: Sterling Publishing Co., 1990.

Pryor, Karen. *Lads Before the Wind*. expanded edition; fourth ed., Waltham, MA: Sunshine Books, 2000.

Reeves, Randall R., Brent S. Stewart, Phillip J. Clapham, and James A. Powell. *National Audubon Society Guide to Marine Mammals of the World*. New York: Alfred A. Knopf, 2002.

Ridgway, Sam, and Richard J. Harrison, eds., *Handbook of Marine Mammals*. *vol. 6. The Second Book of Dolphins and the Porpoises*. San Diego, CA: Academic Press, 1999.

Wilson, Ben. *Dolphins of the World*. Stillwater, MN: Voyageur Press, 1998.

Index

Page numbers in **boldface** are illustrations and charts.

About the Author

DAN GREENBERG is the author of *Whales*, an earlier book in our AnimalWays series. He has also written on a variety of other topics, including spiders, chimpanzees, roller coasters, baseball, frogs, and U.S. history. There are now more than twelve titles in his series of best-selling educational books, including *Comic Book Math* and *Comic Book Grammar*. Greenberg lives in Westchester County, New York, with his wife, two children, and beagle.